Authentically Ashlee

Ashlee Akins

Copyright © Ashlee Akins, 2021

Cover image: © Chocolate Readings

ISBN-13: 978-1-7366962-1-7

Publisher's Note

Printed and bound in the United States of America. All rights reserved. No part of this book may be reproduced or transmitted in any form or by any means, electronic or mechanical, including photocopying, recording, or by any information storage and retrieval system except by a reviewer who may quote brief passages in a review to be printed in a magazine, newspaper, or on the Web without permission in writing from **Ashlee Akins**.

Although the author and publisher have made every effort to ensure the accuracy and completeness of information contained in this book, we assume no responsibility for errors, inaccuracies, omissions, or any inconsistency herein. The advice and strategies contained herein may not be suitable for your situation. You should consult with a professional where appropriate. Neither the publisher nor the author shall be liable for damages arising from here.

Dedication

I want to dedicate this book to mother and my closest friends. In the midst of a pandemic my mom and my besties have been there for me no matter what the situation was. I want to take this moment to thank you all for letting me be me. I know I can be a lot, but you know I mean well and if your truly in my inner circle you know that I love each and every one of you dearly to the moon and back. This book is me from the first page to the last I love you all thank you for excepting my authenticity!

Authentically Ashlee

Table of Contents

Chapter 1
Who is Ashlee?   *7*

Chapter 2
The Pretty "Dark Skinned" Girl   *15*

Chapter 3
Not So Ready to Love   *31*

Chapter 4
Taking L's   *45*

Chapter 5
Love, Oh Love   *63*

Chapter 6
Back to Me   *81*

About the Author   *87*

Chapter 1

Who Is Ashlee?

Let's see… Who am I? It's tough to use one word to describe me. I'm a ball of energy! I'm everybody's bestie. Okay, well, not EVERY body. And depending on who you ask, I could be your worst nightmare or your best dream. It's really no gray area with me. I either love you, or I don't.

Seriously, I try my best not to portray myself to be anybody else. I'm naturally confident, always have been, but I can get a little insecure just like any other woman. I'm a hopeless romantic. I LOVE love. I'm a realist. I love life and all that it has to offer. I love starchy foods. I love my grandmother so much. And I am a child of God. Now, I don't fear any man, but I fear my mama!

Ya'll, my mama is everything! I am not Ashley without Angie.

Yes, she made me add that part…

I'm kidding! My mama is definitely my rock. I wouldn't be where I am without her love, support, and guidance. I can't say who I am without acknowledging her.

Along with me being a mama's girl, I'm a country girl. I'm from Jackson, Tennessee, a small country place where some of the best food, the best fights, the best gospel, and the best churches were established. We have some of the best hairstylists, best-looking women, good-looking men, great athletes, great businesspeople - it's a great country town.

Growing up for me was incredible. I had a strong, hard-working mother that sacrificed her entire life for me, for my grandmother, and she made sure we were both okay. She made sure that I lived a full and fun life. While I knew who my biological father was, I didn't have a relationship with him. Unfortunately, he was in and out of my life.

While I would have loved to have my father around, I was blessed to have an amazing stepfather. He came into my mother's life and swept her off her feet. He helped raise me into the woman I am today, and I am forever grateful for him, and I love him dearly.

As a young girl, my mama kept me busy. I was always singing in the church, in plays, pageants, dance teams, school programs and activities, and after-school programs. I loved the Boys & Girls Club. I used to holler and scream if I couldn't get on that blue bus with Miss Sandra Gill. My entire mission as a girl was to get on that bus and meet up with all of my friends at the Boys & Girls Club. That was a highlight of my childhood.

I loved my elementary school years. I was an excellent student, and I had a lot of friends. I attended Tigrett Middle school for one year, and then my mom decided to transfer me to a magnet school, Jackson Middle. This is where I start discovering who I am. This was when I knew I wanted to tap into my arts and crafts. It was a performing arts school, so in sixth through eighth grade, I got to tap into my creativity. And I LOVED it! It was such an awesome program. They had everything that contributed to my journey's success so far - dance teams, cheerleading teams, chorus, band, and great extracurricular activities. Yeah, that school changed the trajectory of my life.

It was a no-brainer for me to join one of these activities, and I chose the dance team. Once I got to Northside High School, I became a cheerleader. Listen, I got my life as a cheerleader! I had way too much fun. Not only did I cheer all four years, but I was also homecoming royalty. Not sure if you can tell yet, but ya girl was pretty poppin'. I was definitely a popular girl. I know I drove my mom crazy with all of my activities because I was doing my thing from sixth grade to twelfth grade.

Next up – college.

Tennessee State University! Baby, this is where I spent the next four years of my life becoming a woman and I loved every moment of it. Tennessee State shaped me, molded my thought process. It gave me the blueprint to leading my life as a successful, educated, Black woman. Having that HBCU experience taught me the most invaluable life lessons. Learning how to network was key for me. There is where I realized that my network is my net worth. That meant everything to me. Going to TSU taught me how to value my education, my time. I learned how to take charge of my life; how to stand out in a room. Every professional trait you see today, they taught me that. I am forever grateful for that time at TSU. I truly am.

Now, of course, ya girl enjoyed the turn-up! I had a lit social life in college, too. Not only was I Miss Sophomore in Tennessee State

University, but I was also Miss Tiger Gym, Miss Black and Gold runner up, and Miss Congeniality. I was even picked for the meter's favorite for the next Miss Tennessee State University 2008. So, as you can imagine, for me, attending Tennessee State was just an amazing experience. and not only that

While I took pride in being acknowledged for those various platforms, my most memorable platform was being a part of Pom Psi Dance Sorority. Dance is what got me started, so when the opportunity to join a dance team sorority, I was here for it. I was a member of the dance team for four years. I was co-captain and Captain. At some point, I'd become the assistant coach. The people who ran the department saw my passion and encouraged me to try out for the Tennessee Titans. I was good, but I didn't know if I was that good.

Eventually, after being encouraged over and over and over again, I finally tried out. And I'm so glad that I did. I would have never imagined that I'd be a Tennessee Titans finalist, but I was. I was so proud of myself. Now, I didn't make the team, but I still share this accomplishment because I made it so far in the process. Out of about 300 girls to make it to the top 40 while I was still in college. Unfortunately, I didn't make the team because ya girl is a little more melanated than the other girls. At least that was my opinion…

[

Chapter 2

The Pretty "Dark Skinned" Girl

Now, I've known since I was a little girl that I was darker than everyone else. I didn't think anything was wrong with it until someone else thought my skin was a problem. Growing up was difficult because I got called darky, blackie, dirty Q-tip, a lit match- all these different and mean-ass names for being brown skin. To be honest, I didn't think I was that dark. Well, that was until I noticed that everyone around me was lighter than I am, and other people made it a big deal.

My biological father has other children. All his other children are light, except me. So, there were a lot of times where I would hear people compare us. People may think that kids don't pay attention, but oh! Yes, they do. See, I was one of those nosey little girls. You know, always paying attention to grown folks' conversations, ear hustling. And that's when I'd hear them call me names and say, "Oh, she's not that cute" or "Why is she so dark?" It crushed my little spirit. Like, I didn't feel pretty. I wanted to be lighter because, according to adults, those are the cute kids.

Ya know, after hearing over and over again how much better-looking your siblings are, you get used to being the "ugly duckling."

I find it funny how I was teased for being so black, having big lips, and big eyes, yet these are the very features that contribute to me being a beautiful woman.

As an adult, I've mastered how to attract people with my eyes and lips. People tell me how they love my melanin skin. I'm always getting complimented on how milky my skin looks. Can you believe I thought all of this was ugly? Tuh!

It's just sad that sometimes our people tear us down. And this hurtful dialogue came from family or so-called family members and my siblings. My little brothers, of course, never said anything. But my sister and I, it's no surprise that we don't get along. We're not the best of friends or the best of family. It was always a comparison thing between us. She looked different than I did. Her skin was the right shade of light. I didn't feel pretty when I stood next to her. I didn't feel like I belonged when I was with my family. I just felt like I always looked different. I was made to feel like that, and I didn't understand why.

Since my mom was a beautiful, brown-skinned woman, I decided that I can be pretty like her, too. She was confident about her skin, so I can also be confident about mine. It took me a while, but I told myself that I couldn't let those people's opinions of me cloud my judgment.

Now, I may have found my confidence, but that didn't stop the boys from thinking I was ugly! Growing up, kids are cruel. The boys went for the lighter-skinned girls by default. And you know, eventually, I started to get the "You're pretty for a dark skin girl" or "Aw you're so pretty for a little black girl" or "Cute little black."

Oh! And I can't forget the infamous: "You so dark and lovely."

I could never just be pretty. It always had to be an adjective in front of my pretty, and I never understood that at all.

I'm about to be Petty Betty, but um, you know when you're a woman who has a very hairy father, and you inherit that trait, it sucks. One thing that I do appreciate about my extra melanin is that my lil' girl 'stache doesn't show.

Ha!

So yeah, as I got older, I started to appreciate this melanin. It's resilient! I'm thankful, but it did take me time. Honestly, even now at 33 years old, people still come to me saying that silly shit about being pretty for a black girl. Even white girls walk up to me talking about my skin complexion like I'm an art exhibit. I will never understand why people do this to me. It's just skin. Fuck out here.

I've grown just not to let those words hurt. But I mean, it does kind of open up some old wounds of my childhood and knowing that's what I used to hear growing up, and it's still going on today thirty years later, I still hear it. You know, so it is what it is now. As I became an adult, I'm not going to say it was better. But people became freer and slicker at the mouth. Like they don't whisper it no more like they come out and tell you you're pretty for dark skin girl, or and will have the nerve to talk to you about your skin complexion, and let you know that they love your brown skin your melanin, your skin is so smooth!! Crazy shit, right?? I just never understood that. But this is when I understood it...

Colorism is Real AF

I heard of colorism growing up, but I didn't experience it until I was in college. Whenever I tried out for semiprofessional and professional teams to become a cheerleader or dancer, they would often put black girls against black girls. The white girls would be all bunched up together on the side, while all the black girls would have to fight to death for a spot. We had to dance it out against our fellow black girls to be the best black girl, and I used to hate that. We all can't just be great; we have to be the best black girl on the team. Or let's say that it's three ladies with the same name or style but are different shades of brown. They would put all the ladies against each other. And you know who's going to win… the lighter complexion black girl because she's closer to the white girls. Hey, that's just the way it goes down. Or the way it went down.

So yeah, out of forty-something ladies, it might be ten black girls on a team after everyone is chosen. I never understood that no matter how good we were, why couldn't there just be a whole team of us? Because no offense, some of those girls that were Caucasian just couldn't hang with us… some could!! I mean, we were dancers, performers and looked damn good in a uniform. So, I just couldn't understand why we weren't chosen. And I'm speaking for numerous Ashlees and numerous little black girls out there. Because I've been there. I know that I was good. I've made it to the top forty, and low and behold, but I was not chosen. And it wasn't because of my dancing ability. It was because it was going to be too many of us, and I'd be asked to try out next year. Or they'd ask, "Can you lose some weight?" Okay, fine. I'll play the game. I'll lose weight, and then I'll come back and not make the team again. But you're picking white girls that have no talent…

Yeah, mmmkay.

The Exception to the Rule

I quickly learned in this industry that it's all about who you know. It's not about what you can do or how good you are but rather who can put you in a position to get what you want. What's that exception for black girls? Being light-skinned or well connected… period.

Unfortunately, lighter-skinned black women get jobs easier, promotions faster, marry quicker, chosen first – all because they are the exception to the rule. A darker complexioned woman has to do double to get an honorable mention.

People may either not be ready for this conversation or really don't care; either way, it needs to be said. Just because someone's skin is lighter doesn't make them pretty. Can we please stop this? Like now?

Some dope women miss out on incredible opportunities because they're not the exception to the rule of being a black woman. Like, we really have no control over the pigment of our skin. Let's go ahead and put this thing to rest because it's so tiring.

I've missed out on opportunities because I didn't have the right shade of brown or know the right people. It was harder for me to get chosen to be a part of a team. It discouraged me from trying out. I tried out for the Falcons cheerleaders, the Tennessee Titans, and the Hawks. I made it to the very end each time and didn't get chosen. Damn, that pissed me off! You know, I'm a millennial, so I would think that people would not look at the color of my skin but rather look at what I can bring to their organization. I know I'm a dope-ass dancer. In my opinion, there was no other reason to cut me other than me being black. Yea, I said it and so! It didn't matter how great of a dancer I was. that wasn't the case. That wasn't the case in my own family. And that wasn't the case in this whole entertainment world.

While I hated that I didn't make any of those teams, I noticed that more black women are now a part of numerous!! [e1] it's becoming more urban. And you know, I'm glad that they're taking the proper steps towards the future and letting everybody be a part of the team. I fucking love it.

Embracing My Skin
As I'm growing into a woman, I'm embracing my skin color. I love my skin color. I know the world loves my skin color—everybody's melanin popping and pro-black. Put your fist up! We are everything and everywhere! But Everyone is taking a piece of our culture. We're seeing so much cultural appropriation; it doesn't make any sense.

So hey, in my mind, I thought since our culture is being ripped off and people are pretending to accept us as we are, there clearly won't be any problems with me joining a reality show about finding love. Accept me as a single black woman wanting love y'all! Hell, y'all accept everything else! Whew, chile. So, there I was, being vulnerable. I really want love. Soooo Here's my chance. Now Let's see what this is about… okay, y'all sooooo I do the show. The first thing the world wants to do is put me against the light skin girl. Really? I couldn't believe that was happening. Oh, but it did. Listen, when I tell you that good ole internet tore me the fuck down. Whew, chile! They were more worried about the color of our skin rather than him choosing a woman. They were saying shit like, "Oh, actually, he doesn't even like dark-skinned girls," and "You tried too hard" and "He's not attracted to dark skin girls."

People are crazy as hell! I even had someone say, "You're the second dark-skinned girl he's ever been with. He normally dates fair skin and mixed women." I used to hate when people say that shallow shit to me. As if I'm supposed to be grateful that fool chose me. Hell, I have a decision to make too, the fuck! Like the men were the only ones. Uhh no. The sarcastic side of me wanted to ask those assholes, "Do you want a cookie? Am I supposed to jump up and down pissed? Should I be super mad and fly around the room? Honey bye!

At the end of the day, women are women, and men are men. I mean, whether you're black, white, Asian, Hispanic, whoever you are, we're still a man and a woman. I've never looked at someone's skin and judged them based on their skin. And even in 2018, the internet tried to tear us down as black women. It was colorism at its finest.

They try to pin all the light-skinned girls against the dark-skinned girls; they say dumb shit like the light-skinned girls were more beautiful than the dark-skinned girls. And I mean, not only was it embarrassing, but it was depressing. And it's not going to make me self-conscious because I'm very confident. But it did make you kind of look at yourself like, Am I not pretty? Am I not as pretty as her? Because I don't have freckles. Or because, you know, my hair isn't as soft as hers. Or it's because my melanin is too poppin', and I need to tone it down. Do I need to get skin cream and look lighter? And then I have to say, girl, at the end of the day you love you, and you don't disappoint you. So, don't let anybody else disappoint you. If they don't like you, that's their prerogative. Everybody is entitled to their own opinion. They don't have to enjoy all of this beautiful melanin. But I came from a beautiful mom and a wonderful dad, and I'm not going to let anybody make me feel less than, but it definitely fucks with my psyche. Because you would think people wouldn't do that in this day and age, especially trying to pit women against each other. We're trying to build this sisterhood without the bs. That was the part where it hurt. Because you would think that people just don't think to pin women against each other, I mean, you would think they realize that we are trying to obtain our goals. But people are gonna talk regardless. Just don't bring that shit to me. Don't mention my skin complexion. Don't talk about my body or dumb shit that doesn't make sense. Sometimes everything you're thinking does not have to be said, and people need to realize when to shut the fuck up.

    A man is attracted to what's on the inside and the outside. So, you can like a little bit of everything. Like come on y'all, we all know this. In my situation, He clearly doesn't have a type. He likes women. So, he chose light and dark big deal. Beyoncé ring the alarm. But the messed-up part is, the drama and bs came from my brothers and sisters online. YouTube sometimes can be the devil. And I tried to read those messages. But baby, that right there was on a whole different level. Y'all be crazy and bold behind those keyboards, baby. Basically, colorism has just followed me all my life, from childhood to adulthood. I'm always going to be the pretty Brown Girl or the pretty dark-skinned girl. Lol, I don't know why and really don't know how to explain it. But I'm always going to be me, Ashlee. And at this point, I don't accept it; I correct people.

I still hesitate when they say that, but babe, every moment is a teachable moment. And I don't care how old you are. If you feel that you could say something like that, then be prepared for what I have to say after that. I try to teach everybody about colorism every chance I get. It's just certain things you should know. 1. If you don't have anything good to say, don't say it at all. 2. If you have to question what you're about to say before you say it, don't say it because hell, if you feel like it might be uneasy, it's uneasy. That's not something you should say, boo boo. Like you don't tell a pregnant woman damn you're big as fuck.

Come on. Don't say that. Just say you're beautiful. The moral of the story, if you say I'm pretty, I'll tell you the same. I promise not to say who you look good for a brown-skinned girl/guy. Or you look good for a mixed girl/guy you must take after your day. Like nobody says that. Like, it's madness, people. Cut that shit out, mane. Do better, be better, please, and thank you.

Chapter 3

Not So Ready to Love

If someone told me that I'd be on a reality show one day, I'd crack the fuck up! I love being on camera but didn't see myself on camera for this type of show. But there I was, putting my relationship status all the way on blast and letting the world know that I was ready to love.

Okay, so here's how I ended up on the show. I had been on the internet kind of searching for things to do, you know, looking into careers, and I wind up looking up some casting calls. I saw a few that were interesting, and Ready to Love was one of them. I applied and didn't think anything of it. A couple of months go by, and I get an email. It seems like they were a little interested in me, so I told my mom about it. I remember her giving me the third degree: are they asking for money? What are the details? She has to see it in writing first. I had to explain. I'm like, "No, Mom, this is a situation where I can make money and potentially be on TV." She was like, "Okay, we'll just keep it up." So, after reading the email, I realized they were following up to let me know they wanted to do some Skype interviews. They wanted to interview my family and friends to ask specific questions about me.

I couldn't believe it!

I was just playing around on the internet, and then BAM! Your girl is prepping to be on TV. Eventually, they did a couple of Skype interviews with my friends. I also had to submit a video talking about why I should be on the show and all of that. Sounds like an easy and straightforward process, right?

Nah...

The process went on for about eight months. And if that wasn't long enough, the final piece was an in-person interview that lasted about eight hours. This is when they are supposed to get all up in people's business and find out who they truly are. The interview included IQ tests; we spoke to psychiatrists; it was either psychiatrists or psychologists to make sure we weren't loopy and sane enough to be on television.

Oh, and that wasn't it.

We also had to sit in front of eight to ten different producers from numerous shows. We had to go through all of these grilling interviews. Some people laughed; some people cried – it was a lot. I went through an extensive process to be on the show.

There was a point when I thought to myself, whoever they pick is going to be elite because we jumped through hoops to be here! And hopefully, the best of the best is actually ready for love. Me not knowing that in this industry, everything isn't what it seems to be. Some people are around just for the opportunity to be on TV. But then I learned that some people are there because they genuinely wanted to be there.

Lights, Camera, Action!
I get the confirmation that I'm chosen. What?! Me?! I couldn't believe it. The process was so long that I started to get a little impatient. I had to push it to the back of my memory bank because I didn't want to keep emailing or being too eager. To be honest, I'm usually that girl that makes it to the last point and doesn't get chosen. I was in all kinds of disbelief. Since I

really didn't think I would be chosen for the part or be cast, I was just happy to know the wait was over. But I was nervous, anxious, and excited to be on the show.

I remember the day I got the call. I was at home with my best friend, Cameron, just hanging out! A typical Friday night for us, including having dancing music, rapping!! We had our little cocktails. Oh, and eating snacks. So, we were just doing the typical best friend thing. We were sitting on the couch ke-keing, and I got a phone call. And I was like, is this a machine?? And you know, I thought it was a bill collector. I was going to say something witty because it was after seven o'clock. Just as I was about to pop off, the caller says, "Are you ready to love?" I'm like, "Excuse me?"

I was expecting some big ol' grand gesture when they decided to contact me, but that wasn't what I got at all. It was a brief call that was straight to the point. The caller continued, "You've been casting for this show. It's going to be on the OWN network." When I tell you, I fell to the floor in tears, you would have thought I won a million dollars. I was so happy that for once in my life, something happened to me. And I said, "Lord, look at

You showing up and showing out." Not only am I going to be on a television show, but I'm going to be working with Oprah and Will Packer. Like, I don't know how else I could top it like the two most prominent people in the industry right now. She's running everything. He's dominating the industry, especially in Hollywood movies. I was just glad to be chosen. It was the best day of my life. It was the best moment of my life.

After I got the details from the caller, I immediately called my mom. While I would love for my mom to be excited like my friends, her momager hat quickly jumps on the scene, and she puts that thang on. Before the excited, congratulatory response from my mom, I have to give her the run-down on the business when I called her. So, I said, "Yeah, we get paid. Yeah, we on TV." And in true fashion, my mom called our attorney.

While my mom got the business details worked out, I called all my friends. It felt good being supported. Everybody was just happy. Hearing "You deserve it" made my night. Everybody was so excited for me.

Now, after the excitement wore off, it was time for me to buckle down and get myself ready for a new love. Sounds easy to do, right?

Nah…

Not for me! Your girl was so nervous. The very first day, I fucked up. I couldn't even open up the damn door! Now, you know, we got a nice sized house where I live, and I've always lived in a decent area. But I don't open mansion doors frequently, so hey, I messed up a little.

Although a sista tripped on her own feet, I didn't let that ruin my confidence or my night. And when I say trip, I mean, I looked like I couldn't open the door, so I fell into it, tripped. I didn't have time to be embarrassed, so I walk in to see a person greet me with a glass of champagne. I saw beautiful people mingling, and me, I'm a people person. So, I was just ready to go and be myself, and that's what I did.

In the first couple of episodes, I was just being Ashlee, letting people get to know me. I knew that it was a competition to win each other's love, but I had to be fair and give the man in question the opportunity to get to know everybody, not just me. Yes, I'm ready to love, but I need to be, you know, ready for whatever. I understand that you have to be friends first, and I was prepared for that. So, I just went into the situation with an open mind.

And yeah, I was very nervous.

I was one of the youngest ones there, and that was a little intimidating. I wanted people to take me seriously, but I also wanted people to see my sense of humor, understand that I'm a safe zone, and I'm somebody that's going to be a breath of fresh air when I come around. I didn't want to stir the pot. I just wanted to win. I mean, we already have the cameras in our face, so in my mind, I thought, let's not be extra.

So, I tried to keep it light. I just wanted to be Ashlee, and that's how it was each day. Now, I ain't gonna front like it didn't get tense at times. It was a house filled with women. Of course, you know, little moments popped off; women sizing you up. Everybody tries to figure everybody out. And I hope I don't get in trouble saying this, but when it comes to women, you put a bunch of women in the room, the older women are going to size up the younger women, they're going to say that they're instantly going to put you in their little sister mode. For whatever reason, they don't view you as competition. Some women feel like they're better off not having friends than just trying to get to know people. So that's why I went in as Ashlee. I want to get to know each individual, but who they were instead of who their representative was. So, you got to kind of break those barriers there. That's what I did.

Don't Play With Me
Now, as I said, I tried my best to be cool with the ladies on the show, but sometimes there's always one that gotta try you. And I had to let her know I am not the one to be tested. This one particular classmate just gave me a hard time. She was one of those individuals who have an opinion of everything. She always has something to say. And it might not be the nicest thing either. For whatever reason, she was always picking on me, and I got tired of it.

This particular day we were filming, and she said something smart, and I just had to get at her at that moment. I told the crew I'm about to pull up. I sent out a message live while we were filming. Okay, I erased it… I needed to act right. But y'all, I wanted to talk to her and let her know babee we could finish this conversation in person. For a min, I wasn't trying to hear none of that shit! I said, "I want to see you say whatever you just said on the phone, to my face!" And you know, for a minute, I lost myself. I forgot where I was. All of a sudden, I hear God whisper to me, Don't embarrass your mama. Usually, I would never do anything to embarrass my mom. But that day ya'll, I had time!

People are quick to judge people for popping off without understanding why they popped on. For me, it was the disrespect, over and over (and over) again. What I don't like is for someone to talk to me like I am one of their children. I can't give respect where respect isn't given. I really wish adults understood this concept. Just because someone is younger does not give you a pass to be rude. Bottom line, when you are disrespectful, you will get disrespect. It's very simple.

At that moment, I felt the need to pop off because she kept trying me. The woman I am today wouldn't even entertain any foolishness like that. I finally am to the point where I had to realize, hey, Ashlee, everybody's not going to like you. Everybody's not going to be on your side; you have to understand when it's time to pick and choose your battles. And that day, I had to choose my battles. And my battle wasn't with her. It was with myself.

I had to decide to stop giving my power away to people who don't matter to me. I'm popping, and I'm great when people see that they try to pick with you. She was hating, period. I had to let that go in true Ashlee fashion with my three favorite words: Girl, fuck you!

After that incident, I kept moving. The show's atmosphere was so much fun; it was hard for me to stay in a funk. I definitely couldn't stay mad after I connected with my big sis, Shea!! The cabin trip we took was one of the best moments we had. We cried we laughed, we got to know each other, and it was so dope. It came down to the wire where we had to understand that our going on the show was much bigger than finding a man. We women came together, and we fell in love with ourselves and fell in love with each other. We understood that sometimes young men don't have it all. We all know that we're great catches.

So, it was a breaking point for all of us to take the competition out.

The Man I Thought I Was Ready To Love
My first thoughts of Alex when I saw him was damn! I thought he was a fine tall glass of chocolate milk. He was fine enough to quench my thirst. He was like water, and I wanted to stand by the water cooler every day. Not only was he fine, but he was cool. He was slick. He had that Chicago swag. I liked him because he had a little hood in him, but he was such a gentleman. He didn't judge me. He would get my drink before I would even ask for it. He would also hold the door open for me. Get my chair. He always knew what to say, exactly how to compliment me.

Apparently, that wasn't enough because that man sent me through hell. I can't believe all of the things that I had to experience, but I know that it helped mold and shaped me into the woman I am today - a challenging but necessary lesson. Like they say: sometimes you win, and sometimes you lose, and when it came to that situation, I definitely lost.

Chapter 4

Taking L's

Whew child! Let me tell ya'll! Taking loss after loss after loss will break a sista all the way down. It's not easy dealing with the blows of life back-to-back to back. And that's exactly how I felt after everything that went down with me. Now, I'm a southern girl, so you know I grew up in church, God, and the bible. Prayer is always something I had, but at that moment, I can honestly say that I didn't even know how to pray anymore.

I knew that I wasn't feeling like myself, but I didn't realize just how low my faith was until the holidays rolled around. I love the holidays, and I'm always looking forward to Thanksgiving and Christmas, but I was not feeling the holidays this particular season of my life, and rightfully so. A lot was going on, and I had no clue how to juggle it all. Even though people love the show, fans are rolling in; everything appears to be great - I'm depressed. I'm fake smiling and trying to laugh at jokes that aren't even funny. I mean, I'm just trying to do everything to make my life appear to be better.

But inside, I was dying. I felt empty. I was lying about my reality, and I didn't know how to pray my way out of it. In my mind, I was doing the right thing for so long, but then I also find out that maybe I wasn't praying the right way or explicitly asking for what I wanted.

I just felt like I didn't know how to talk to God anymore. I felt like He wasn't listening to me. I felt like everybody misunderstood me, and when I say everybody, I mean everybody. I felt like people were saying things I wanted to hear instead of what I needed to hear. So, at this point, I had to seclude myself from everybody. I had to kind of fall into my own sunken place. But I didn't want to stay there and knew that God would be the only one to bring me out. I still felt a way about talking to God, and then something just came over me. I said to myself, "You know what, I'm gonna do it my way. I'm gonna talk to God the way I know-how. And I'm going to keep it real; I need to say what I need to say, say it how I wanna say it, and talk to Him like He is my friend and He's gonna accept me. I know He wants me to be me and stop being someone else now."

And that's exactly what I did.

So, I'm like: "Listen, bro, God, I've come to you as broken as I am. I've never been this broken than at this moment in my life. I don't know if I am supposed to even be in a marital relationship. All I want is for You to heal me. I need You to help me understand myself better because it takes two to tangle so, I can't blame everybody; I have to blame myself to help me grow. So, teach me how to walk better, teach me how to think better. You know, help me make better decisions, stop letting me be so bullheaded that I think that I'm doing it right, and stop letting me be a follower and pretend like things are okay because half of the other world it's that what they are doing."

So yeah, I just really had to talk to God and start clearing motherfuckers out of my life. And when I began praying for negativity, for fake people, and for people who don't mean any world to get away from me, I had many lonely moments. Often, I had to go back to my lonely childhood being the only child, talking to myself, entertaining myself. I had to get to know me! That was the stance I needed to take because I didn't know who I was and be somebody that I'm trying to be this influencer and I'm trying to tell people the good, positive joys of life. I didn't believe it. So, I had to go back, resurface and date Ash. I had to date myself, I had to date God, and I had to learn how to talk to Him. I don't know how everybody else prays. I don't know that blah, blah, blah. But I know how to speak to Him and tell Him what I want, what I need, and thank Him for the simple things.

See, that's what a lot of people forget. We forget that we don't wake up on our own. We don't move our fingers on our own. Blessings don't come from you. They come from somebody above you or higher than you. So, when I started appreciating the small things, He does for me and the baby steps and actually being happy for those baby steps, I feel that I have stopped doubting myself for not feeling enough. I had to start slapping myself on the back for every small accomplishment. "Look at God!"

There's a saying, "Give people their flowers while they're alive," so I give myself flowers and my God flowers for me to get out of that dark place and ready to learn, grow and evolve.

Being On TV Ain't All That

Everybody thinks when you are on TV that life is excellent. You got maids, and you get money every month. You're living lavish, you have luxury cars, and people open the door for you, but that is not the damn truth, mmmkay?

Many people living in these lives that we see online and on television are miserable because they do not have a relationship with themselves or with God. They are too busy trying to impress you, and that's where I was losing myself trying to impress the world instead of making myself happy, impressing God, and impressing myself. So, it took me time to know that I was the problem, and it took me time to get back into a place where I could talk to God like a normal person. I had to trust God and had to trust that the path might be lonely. And it was, but I needed it.

I haven't been in a relationship since I broke up with ol' boy. I have dated people, but I don't call those relationships. Those were just dates. It's been a couple of years since that tragic shit, and mentally I am in a way better place than I was when I left that show. I'm in a much better space now than when I lost my faith in God. I can own my shit and talk to God and not being embarrassed about who I am and what I have done. And you know not to be embarrassed to not know what my future holds and where my future lasts. I don't make those long-term plans anymore. I don't do all of that. I don't put all of that stress on my life anymore. I do real things. I set weekly goals instead of monthly goals and yearly goals because you will get depressed if you don't make it. So, I set the baby steps for myself. It might not work for everybody else, but I have to do what's best for me.

    I started living in my truth, in my life and doing things that I say, and actually being happy with my actions. I think that's why I was able to talk to God and not be afraid and ashamed to talk to Him. I didn't forget to thank Him. You know, a lot of times, I was moving and thinking that I was doing it on my own, but it wasn't me. It was Him at all times. So, I had to just sit back, relax, and focus on the most important: me and God and my relationship with Him.

Pulling Myself Out of The Darkness

Since I'm not made for depression, I was ready to get back to my bubbly self after a while. So, I started taking the necessary steps to get better. I had to stop reading the negative comments about me. I hated it all the time, but that is rule number one. When you are in the spotlight, don't you dare go back and forth with these viewers and fans. Don't become mad, and they don't matter if you don't read them. I am the type of person who likes to respond to people not negatively but to let them know that I am normal. I wanna talk to you. I don't wanna feel like I'm the megastar that can't say hi and thank you when you dish out a compliment. But the negative stuff, you just have to let it go. That was step one for me. Well, you know what, that was step two.

I actually have to say that step one was forgiveness. I don't know if anybody has been so mad that you feel like it's your side action. I wanted to whoop Alex's ass! Like I wanted to whoop... his... ass. Because I thought that I had talked to a grown man and I had told that grown man don't you lie to me and embarrass me, but you did the same thing and did it on purpose with a fucking smile on your face. But I had to forgive him. Because it's not my fault that he doesn't know how to love a woman properly, it's not my fault that he doesn't know how to be a good friend. That's on him and God. He gotta deal with God, not me, because I'm not in control of his actions or life. So, once I forgave him, I could move on mentally because he had me in jail in my mind. I was doing all good and portraying it on the outside, but I was fighting him on the inside every day on death row. Every single day, we would fight. I don't care where it was. I was fighting him, and I had to quit fighting him to for me to forgive him. So, step one for me was to forgive him.

Another part of step two for me was to learn to ignore the bullshit, the background noise. Everybody in my ears tried to give me advice, and I had to let their advice go saying I don't need your advice. The only advice I'm gonna take is my mom's. That's it. Everybody else is not needed. Sorry. I just had to focus and get all of the naysayers and extra baggage out of my life.

So then, I started to lose friends, associates. So, that's was like step three.

Some of the naysayers were my friends, so I was social distancing before social distancing. I had to socially distance myself from certain people who kept putting me in a destructive mindset or put me in a situation to make me think negatively about certain things.

Then there comes ignoring men. I had to ignore men for a while. I'd let them know that I don't wanna go on a date. I'm not fit to go on a date. Mentally, I'm not there. I had to separate myself from the dating scene because I knew I wasn't 100% ready to give myself to another man. Because I felt like you all keep fucking playing with me. So why am I gonna prepare myself to give myself to be none other than just a play? So, I had to do that.

I had to take away social media a little bit. Not just reading the comments but just getting off it. Just get off it. I was not even posting on holiday. I couldn't keep pretending anymore. I decided that I couldn't be everywhere. I can't be at all the red-carpet appearances. I didn't want to be fake anymore.

So, I think those processes and those baby steps like pulling away from people, meditating, taking time out to know me, figuring out my flaws, figuring out what to work on, reading a little more. And then I started writing a little bit more, writing my music. Putting my emotions on paper and saying stuff, folding it up, tearing it up, and getting rid of it. Once I write it down, and I'm done with it. I just had little steps to make myself feel better. And it worked. Once I received clear instructions on moving forward, I was able to walk on the right path. At least I think it's right; I feel that it is right.

So, after getting all the background noise out, praying more, reading more, and being more honest with myself, I finally decided to talk to my mother about it. She had already known that I was going through all this, but she says that she didn't say anything. She said, "I've been worried about you, baby, and I'm glad that you are admitting that something is wrong. This is something that can be a teaching moment for everybody. Everybody gets depressed, everybody goes through stuff, but I'm glad that you were able to figure this out and just know that I'm always here."

As adults, we know that we have our parents with us, but sometimes we wanna do things independently. I didn't want my mom's experience to cloud my judgments. I wanted my own experience, and I wanted to figure it out like a big girl. Because, as I say, we live and die alone. I don't need her to tell me how to do every single thing. She was proud that I took the time away to figure out my problems on my own and figure out different methods of making me feel better. And then I started to be vocal about it. That really helped me, telling the truth. Telling people what they don't wanna hear.

I just had to tell people the truth, and once I started telling the truth and taking the steps and just keeping it real with myself, keeping myself away from the bullshit, I started to feel better and started to look better. I started to gain my weight back and started to feel sexy again. The acne was gone. The trauma was elevated from my life. Sometimes, I think that my life is more boring because I don't have any drama anymore. I had to sit back and thank God and say, "Hey! You are the thing. You are the person I need to thank for this because, without You, I still would have been more screwed." So, that was what it is.

Connecting with God Be Like…
On my journey to getting to know God again, I fell in love with connecting with Him in my own way. My favorite way is finding a quiet place and finding a place where nobody else is and talking to Him out loud—cracking jokes and being myself 100%. I don't care if it's a closet, bathroom, downstairs, outside in the yard, or deep in the woods. I don't care where it is; I just need to be alone.

Once I'm alone, I can talk to Him and say what I wanna say and cry. Wherever I am, I'm gonna talk to Him. I'm gonna take my time to give Him enough respect so I can have a one-on-one conversation with Him. And that's what a lot of times people forget that you have to give Him that respect, give Him that time. Move away from everything else, and you gotta only focus on what you and God are talking about.

And that's what I did Wherever I am, I find a nice quiet place, and I take my time so I can have a conversation with Him. And next thing, He hears me. And I yell if I feel like He ain't listening. I cry if I feel like He ain't listening. So, I pray until I get an answer.

When I talk to God, it makes me feel as if I'm taking a burden off me, and I'm giving it to Him. Because He doesn't want me to worry, he doesn't want me to stress. And that's the whole point of having a mustard seed of faith. That's how I keep my faith. Whatever problem I have, I'm gonna give it to God, okay. Like I don't know when I'm going back to the school system, so I'm going to hand it to you. And the next thing you know, here I am writing another book. Here I am getting deals done. Here I am, getting ready to go on a new show. Every time I hand it to Him, he figures out a way to make me come back on top. That's what I do. I give everything to God, no matter what it is.

Bouncing Back From Defeat
Listen! If somebody had told me all of the heartache, disappointments, let-downs, and bad days I'd experience trying to pursue my

goals, I don't know if I would have gone through with it. I've experienced soooo many L's that it's hard to jump into something new without knowing for sure I'll come out on top. But life has taught me that no matter how prepared you are, you'll experience defeat in some way, shape, or form.

Because I've had to bounce back more times than I care to remember, I know how to do it more quickly when it does happen – oh, because it will happen. Even to you. Have you ever fallen off but didn't have the knowledge, strength, or tools to get back up? That was me until I went through the mess. So! If I had to share what I would do when it's time to bounce back, here's what I'd tell you to do:

- ✓ The first way to bounce back from defeat is to admit that you've been defeated. We have to admit that we've lost, okay, we have to admit it. I know it's hard, but the truth will set you free.
- ✓ Secondly, figure out what the hell you did wrong and how you can fix it the next time. Remember, there's nothing new under the sun, so you'll face a

similar situation. This time, you'll know what to do.
- ✓ And the third way is executing it to the point where you leave no errors or room for errors or mistakes. Do you and go hard.

We believe in what we are doing and practice and re-practice and re-practice it to the point where it's no flaws. So again, understanding and accepting the defeat, figuring out how to prevent that defeat from re-occurring, and figuring out other methods of making it better. Believe in yourself so you will not ever be defeated again.

Chapter 5

Love, Oh Love

Okay, so here's the thing, I definitely want to be in love. It's a beautiful feeling to have somebody you connect with, you know. But I have to be honest, some days, I feel blessed that I sleep well at night, and I don't have to worry about anything going on with my partner. I don't have to have those stresses about him looking at this big booty girl on Instagram or taking this girl on a vacation, you know. So, some days are good, then some days are horrible. Some days I hate it here! I'll be having one of those men ain't shit moments, and then I'll go outside and everybody and they mama in love that day. I can't go anywhere without seeing people all in love and shit. I mean, from the dogs to that cats, the grandparents, like everybody holding hands and kissing and touching booties and stuff, and I ain't got nobody to touch. Days like that, I hate being single.

For the most part, I'm happy about my relationship status because I hear all these horror stories about relationships and failed marriages. But at the end of the day, everybody wants someone. So, it's not like I am planning to be single. It's just the people that I choose have not been the right ones for me. And I'm working on picking the right person and not really picking but letting him come to me because whatever the hell I'm doing is wrong. So, you know, I'm just kind of feeling a little left out at this point. After going on a dating show that I thought was going to be, you know, my way to getting married and finding out that he was a fucking frog, that damaged my confidence. That fool had no intentions of being with anybody but himself. Going through that was embarrassing.

To be honest, I think that might be another reason men are afraid to date me because I had a relationship, and it went basically viral. And they think that our relationship is probably going to do the same and it's not going to work. But I mean, I don't know, maybe I'm too picky. I'm just, I'm happy, but I'm not happy. I want someone, but I want someone to want me if that makes any sense. I want to just want someone to be the only person I want. Does that make sense?

So yeah, I'm trying to do it right this time! Be patient and shit. And let me let you - that shit is boring! It's depressing. I spend a lot by myself. I am trying my best to have a good attitude while I wait. You know, oh, yeah, cool. I'm just patiently waiting on this right! Knowing damn well, I can't wait for Mr. Right to knock on my door. He can ask me to go to the gas station with him, and I'm going, you know!

At this point, I vowed to be more open about the men I choose to date. To not be so shallow, to consider things that actually matter when finding the right person. But at the same time, I can't pretend like a sista ain't getting up there in age now! The older I get, I keep thinking my clock is starting to tick. I'm not that young. I need to have a baby. I'm in my mid-thirties. I'm starting to get nervous. Like, am I going to be single forever? Do I need to go ahead and start collecting dogs and cats? Like, is it going to just be me and my pets?

Being single in my mid-thirties with no children is starting to kind of make me feel like I'm not complete. And yes, I know that I don't need a man to complete me. But, I'm used to seeing that in my household. I feel safe, loved, protected, cared for when I'm surrounded by love and family. That's what marriage is to me. Not just about having a man but sharing my life with someone that I love and care for. You know?

For me, it's only right that I have someone to share my life with, but this waiting game is just stressful. Either I meet men that aren't as cool as me or everybody that I like, don't like me, and the people who want me, I don't like them back. It's weird! This waiting game is challenging. It's no easy way to put it. Being single can get complex and even cause a sista to get a little thirsty.

Oh, don't act like you haven't been thirsty, sis! I know I have. A lot of times. First of all, let me define what me being thirsty looks like. Okay, sometimes I buy certain outfits and go to certain places just because I know it will be men there. Because I mean, I just want somebody to talk to me. And you touch my hair. You know, flirt with me.

I was so thirsty for this one person that I lightweight stalked him. Well, okay, you can decide if I stalked him or not, but I heard about an event he was hosting. He didn't invite me, so um, I basically invited myself. So, when I got to the event, I sat in a corner waiting for that person to get there. When I saw him, I wind-up messaging that person on Instagram. Like hey, I see you. And he was like, "Oh my God, where are you at?" I was like, "Oh, I can't believe we're in the same place!" Knowing damn well my thirsty ass did all of that on purpose.

So yeah, I've been thirsty. There have been times where I had to slap myself and say, "Come on, girl! You're better than that." But yep, I think everyone is thirsty at some point and especially if you like a particular person. Just don't be like me sitting in the damn corner waiting on some damn man to notice you. Quench that thirst!

Friends, No Benefits
I think I struggle with my love life because men always see me as the cool homegirl. And to be honest, it's been my fault. Rather than admitting that I was romantically attracted to men in my past, I played the role of just being his friend, hoping that would blossom into something more.

Looking back, I realized how I allowed certain things to occur just because I wanted to be around that person. Like, allowing myself to hang out with him and his homeboys. You're playing the game, and I know damn well I'm bored, but you want me to sit there while you play? Yeah, I'm going to be a high-fiving you after every win. Yeah, if you're on Instagram and see a pretty girl, I'm going to act like I'm not fucking intimidated. Even though that girl looks like Beyonce on fucking steroids. Like, she looks even better than me. I'm not going to hate or show my insecurities. Instead, I say, "Oh, she's beautiful." What I should have done is let him know that I was interested in him and felt a way about him looking at other women.

    Doing this caused me to push myself all the way out the way. Me not admitting how I really felt made the guys switch their focus on this other damn girl. Like, what the fuck?! So, it's like, I've done those types of things and basically set myself up for failure. I've learned to be upfront about what I want from a man so I don't have to go through that again because I can't.

Just Right For Me

When it comes to who would be the right man for me, I think of someone who is confident, knows what he wants. He knows who he is, what his purpose is in life. I want to look at my man and feel that I can't like control myself. I want him to make love to my mind. I want someone to just have me; nothing else matters. I want someone who wants us to have tunnel vision, with our result always being us. I want to have a financial partner; I want to have a business partner and my mate. I just want to grow together with the same person. I want to have a whole Bonnie and Clyde best friend situation. I still want to enjoy life and be as young as I can.

    I don't want anybody that always makes these goals, and that's all we're ever doing, trying to make it to this goal. Or we want to get a house, or we want to get this car, or we want to get this business started. Like I don't want to live for that. I will live each day like it's alive. Like I want to spend fifteen minutes in the morning meditating with my head on his chest. And him just talking to me about absolutely nothing or us just breathing and just enjoying that we have each other no matter what. I just want to feel at home when I look at my man's eyes.

I want to be loved. I want to love somebody just as hard as they love me. I don't want to be the only one in love. I don't want to force anything on anybody. I just want it to be fluid, and it just be dope.

I'm a clown, so I want you to be somebody I can clown with, you see. I want somebody I can crack lewd jokes with. I don't care if it's the wrong time. I'm the person that cracks a joke at a funeral. I want him to get me and not let me feel ashamed to be this extrovert, loud person.

And I don't feel like that's too hard to ask for.

I'm Single, So What
Coming from a country town and a country place you know, it's better to be married, especially at my age. A lot of older and more mature women question why I don't have children. They ask why I am not in a long-term relationship or have a mate. I don't even bother trying to answer because I'm living my life; I

am chasing my dreams. But I'll keep it real; I do get lonely.

You know, the character Mary Jane is someone I can relate to. She was single, dated some fine-ass successful men, she was a boss, looked damn good, and sis appeared to have it all together. But at the end of the day, she was lonely.

So, like Mary Jane, I know that I could have everything together, but at times I get lonely too. I just don't want to date out of loneliness. I'm happy where I am. But I also know that I would be more satisfied with a mate. I don't want to say that I'm less, I feel like I'm missing something, or my heart isn't complete. I'm thrilled, and I'm very blessed. But I would be happier and more blessed with someone else.

For now, I'm single… but so what!

Growing Into My Womanhood
So, you know, this whole journey I've been on is all about me growing into the woman I was born to be. And I have to admit, that has not been easy. It's hard to own your stuff. At least it was for me at first. Taking responsibility for

the role I've played in failed relationships was a bit challenging. But I have definitely taken responsibility and now own my stuff. I had to be honest with myself and admit that I like fixer-uppers. I like projects. So, I had stopped getting the guys that are dreamers. The ones who talk a good game but don't take any steps to make anything happen. Because I badly wanted to start building a solid relationship, I overlooked important things like that. I only looked at the bigger picture like we can have this, and we'll be in this type of house, and we'll have this type of money in the account. I had to own up to myself and admit out loud, "You love fixer-uppers. You love projects. You love DreamWorks."

Now, please know that I would also try to date guys that had it together. But I think I was running into men that wanted to be my dad. And I hate for people to tell me what to do.

So, yeah, I had to be okay with just being unattached for a while. If I had to give my lil' two cents to other single women, I'd say learn how to be complete on your own. That's what I had to do. And then you can accept whatever type of relationship you want once you have it together. Stop looking for that partner. You will only find fuck boys. Trust me, I know.

I was trying to find the perfect mate. He needed to have his shit together. Bank account on point, own car, house, all of that needed to add up for me. That's what I was going for. So, I had to stop doing that. Then it was, you know, looks. I had to stop doing being shallow. If a man didn't look a specific type of way, I wouldn't talk to him. Then I called myself purposely dating "ugly" men. But I found out the ugly ones are just as trashy as the fine ones. They do the same thing. And you know, really it was just like trial and error with me. I had to just cut out all of my superficial things. So, here's what I learned about dating:

- ✓ You need to make sure your finances are together.
- ✓ You need to make sure you're mentally stable.
- ✓ You need to make sure you have what you're asking for.
- ✓ You can't expect these things if you can't give these things.

Once I owned up to that and started living in my truth, my perspective on dating changed. I realized that I had to relearn myself, date myself. Bless myself, treat myself. I started to appreciate who I was as a woman. I started living life, actually being happy. Now that I'm happy, I've been meeting quality men.

Now to say I like them all would be a whole lie. But I have been meeting a different type of man. And I like what I've been seeing. I feel good just about dating. Not being thirsty anymore. You know, I'm not looking for anything. I'm not trying too hard. I'm enjoying myself. Being confident. When I have a conversation, I'm able to admit my flaws and my thoughts. I own my shit. And it feels good to be noticed for that versus just, you know, bullshit.

Part of me growing into my womanhood understands what it meant for me. And for me, being a grown woman is someone who can understand every action does lead to a reaction, and everything doesn't need a rebuttal. A grown woman stays in her own lane. Just living beautifully, minding her damn business, going to work, handling her business, eating good, living and enjoying herself, paying her bills, just being a sister to another sister. I feel like that's the grown woman I am and strive to be. A person that exudes positivity at all times. We all have our moments, but let those dark moments be teaching moments and steppingstones. Grown women don't dwell in those moments. In pity or darkness, grown women can always find a light. That's definitely who I'm trying to be, and I work my bone to try to become and be every day and embody.

Say Ouch! And Move On
Being in love to me is so dope, but that process of falling in love can be a little hurtful. Wanting to be in a loving relationship has definitely had me saying ouch a time or two or ten. Although I've experienced some painful lessons in love, I've had some enlightened ones, too. One of the best lessons I've learned about myself as a single woman is to pay attention to details. Not just in relationships but every area of your life. Noticing small details, aka red flags, will help you avoid hurt, harm, or danger in any fashion.

I remember being at a club with an individual. And he wanted to buy my drinks. My mom always said, "Don't ever let anybody buy your drinks. You get them, or you sit at the bar with them. And you watch that drink from the bartender's hand to his hand to your hand. Or you try your best to reach for it." I tried my best to stick by this. But this particular night, I gave in. The guy I was with kept insisting that he gets a drink. He said he wanted me to relax and chill with my homegirl. Fine. So, I let him get it. I didn't think he was going to do anything to me. So I drank the drink. Within thirty minutes or so after consuming the drink he bought me, I started to feel weird. I began to sweat profusely. I began to feel like I was about to pass out. I started walking, but I couldn't feel my legs. It was like I was dead weight. I was pushing people down, trying to find my balance. I finally made it to security. I said, "Hey, somebody put something in my drink. I can feel it. I feel weird. Something's wrong. Something's wrong with that drink. Can you please get me home? We didn't drive together. I drove alone."

Before the security guard could respond, the guy who put something in my drink came outside. He told the security guard that he had me. I looked at that security guard, and I told him, please don't let me leave with him. I begged him. I said, "I don't know him like that. Do not leave me with him." Then, the girl I was with was so hung up on who the guy was that she didn't even care what was going on. She was on some real group bitch type shit. She was like, "Ashlee, come on. We good. We're good." And I'm like, really? Bitch. I'm telling you, he put something in my drink. And you still want to go with this fool? Like, are you fucking kidding me?

I didn't go with him. I wind up getting sober at the club. They gave me water and everything. And I was able to make it home. Moral of the story: pay attention to your surroundings and pay attention to detail. It'll save you.

I put myself in some challenging situations, but I know that it's helped mold me into a better woman to find a better man and create the relationship that I want.

Chapter 6

Back to Me

One thing I love about life is that you can always start over. We all get to a point where we can turn this around. I'm there in my life. This is the turning point. Ashlee has discovered this new version of her. She has healed from this depressing situation—the turning point. If you're wondering, who is Ashlee today, I'd say that Ashlee is an exciting extrovert, a whole lot of women. Ashlee is the world's best friend. I'm gonna keep it real to you. I'm gonna give it to you raw, but I'll make sure you have a great time in life. I'm gonna support you. I'm just a fancy diva. You'll meet thousands of people, but you'll never meet a person like me.

In a world of everything being so superficial, my authenticity speaks for itself. My personality is fun-loving and jolly. When I walk into a room, I demand attention, and I've been like this since I was a baby. I've been the center of attention. Born in seven months, couldn't even wait to come out of my mama. I had always wanted to be the center of attention. I'm just like the princess of everyone's little fairytales. I bring spunk, bring personality, bring energy, bring uniqueness, and bring style. I'm a protector. I'm a Pitbull. I can give you whatever you give me, but Ashlee is that chick. She is that girl, and most Ashlee's are. We are awesome.

Most people think I'm putting on, but I'm not. I've always been this way. I've always been this girl. I don't know any other way to be. I have always been the life of the party. I'll make everybody laughing. I just know how to make any situation good. And I thank my father for that, my stepfather, cause he had such a way with people. I was already like that with people, but then you live by an example, and he has taught me to make the lightest situation. Why so serious? Everything doesn't have to be so serious. You can also have fun while doing stuff. So, I've always been like this. I have always been extra. I have a loud but soft personality, and I don't know how to change it.

To be honest, I don't plan on changing it. I like everything about me, whether it bothers others or not. I'm just trying to accomplish my life's goals and be authentically me.

So, my only advice for women is to not give a fuck to what everybody else says. Do you all day. That's me, and that's how I'm gonna live. I can't live for anybody else because I'm not going to live my truth if I do that. I have to live for myself, and you should do the same. Handle your business but don't forget that you are an individual while handling your business. So, do you at all cost.

About the Author

Ashlee Akins is a Radio Personality, Reality TV Star, and 2x Author. The vibrant beauty hails from Jackson, Tennessee. Along with obtaining her bachelor's degree in Speech Pathology and Audiology, Ashlee is also an accomplished entrepreneur. She is passionate and excited about her women's empowerment brand, AA Dimensions.

www.ingramcontent.com/pod-product-compliance
Lightning Source LLC
LaVergne TN
LVHW041634070426
835507LV00008B/620